AF413282

A Dance in Medias Res

A Dance in Medias Res

Poems from Transcendent to Immanent

RYAN KEATING

Foreword by Charles Taliaferro

Illustrations by Ruby Keating

RESOURCE *Publications* · Eugene, Oregon

A DANCE IN MEDIAS RES
Poems from Transcendent to Immanent

Resource Publications
An Imprint of Wipf and Stock Publishers
199 W. 8th Ave., Suite 3
Eugene, OR 97401

www.wipfandstock.com

PAPERBACK ISBN: 979-8-3852-0398-7
HARDCOVER ISBN: 979-8-3852-0399-4
EBOOK ISBN: 979-8-3852-0400-7

VERSION NUMBER 11/03/23

For Ness, with whom I dance;
and for Ruby, Jonah, Alev, and Lale in
whom I see God high and low.

CONTENTS

FOREWORD

Ryan Keating's poetic dance in the middle of things is no ordinary dance among ordinary things. True, there are ordinary elements on display—bread, wine, coffee, rocks, even fish tacos—but these are on the cusp of a rhapsodic, creative engagement with the mysteries of Christian faith (the Trinity, the incarnation, God's hiddenness, redemption) and nothing less than a philosophical revelry on space and time. This is no small task, and Keating's taking it on with such virtuosity and humility takes my breath away. A friend once wrote about the difficulty of successfully writing about the supernatural and the ordinary: "Great mystery there. Well, buzz along—Let's not get tremulous and starry-eyed. Here—have a cigarette." I see no such tension in Keating's imaginary in which he is at home reflecting on the Perichoresis (the Greek term for the intimate relationship of the Father, Son, and Holy Spirit as the Holy and indivisible Trinity) as transporting his daughter to take a driving test.

I recently had the pleasure of co-authoring with Ryan a chapter on English thought about God's omnipresence from 1600 to 1900. This involved scholarship on the likes of Isaac Newton and Henry More (like Ryan, a philosopher and a poet) for Oxford University Press. While that work was a book on space, time, and God, intended for scholars, it is such a joy to recommend to you this very different enterprise: a versatile collection of poems that are capacious and potentially transformative. Unlike an academic project, this collection invites readers to personally explore space and time *Coram Deo* (in the presence of God). I read and re-read them in the spirit of those great lines from *For the Time Being: A Christmas Oratorio* by the British poet W.H. Auden:

Space is the Whom our Loves are needed by,
Time is our choice of How to love and Why.

Charles Taliaferro
Emeritus Overby Distinguished Professor, St. Olaf College

ACKNOWLEDGMENTS

"Perichoresis" first appeared in *Saint Katherine Review*

"He Chora Tou Achoretou," "Hiddenness," "Four Wisps," "This Weird Garden," and "Looking for the Kingdom of God" first appeared in *Ekstasis Magazine*

"The Father Gives His Son Cells," "I Speak in Tongues," "Sleep is Trust," "A Psalm for August," "Editing Branches," "Jesus Heals a Paralytic," "Death is At Work" and "The End" first appeared in *Agape Review*

"Presence," "The Wine Remembers" and "Jonah Moves" first appeared in *Foreshadow Magazine*

"To Singing," and "Baby Swallows" first appeared in *Calla Press*

"Make Me and Icon" first appeared in *Macrina Magazine*

"Waiting on Holy Saturday" first appeared in *Fathom Magazine*

"The World in His Hands" first appeared in *Earth and Altar Magazine*

"Ekmek" and "Esther" first appeared in *Inkslinger*

"Elisha and His Servant" first appeared in *Lothlorien Poetry Journal*

"Sinking Jonah" and "Faces of Figs" first appeared in *Clayjar Review*

"He Knows What Lies in Darkness" first appeared in *Wine Cellar Review*

"Natural" first appeared in *Resurrection Mag*

"Rock Collection" first appeared in *Amethyst Magazine*

"For Common Creatures" first appeared in *Overtly Lit*

"Nanaimo" first appeared in *Roi Fainéant*

"Fish Tacos" first appeared in *Anglican Theological Review*

PERICHORESIS

A dance *in medias res*
Our hands and feet together
Cast identical shadows
Of union and uniqueness
In overlapping circles
By common light refracted
Onto the floor of heaven

As earth reflects the pattern
Of perfect indwelling light
My people gather around
In diversity as one
Pushing darkness back again
I take all their hands in mine
And for all the world we dance

HE CHORA TOU ACHORETOU

An ancient mosaic in a church in Istanbul describes
Mary as "The Container of the Uncontainable."

She held within her him who holds
every body in heaven and on earth,

the planets and the people in orbit
around the virgin full of grace

to bear a baby without borders
or boundaries, uncomprehended

inside a fragile vessel favored,
and overflowing for generations

like an infinite vineyard swirling
in her glass and flooding the world

with wine for gladdening human hearts
and saving them from the hour of death.

Mary magnified the Lord and treasured
in her heart the word of God made flesh

who makes space for all of us and speaks
the borders and boundaries and orbits

into place and chose a woman to become
the container of the uncontainable.

HE CHORA TON ZONTON

*An ancient mosaic in a church in Istanbul describes
Jesus as "The Land of the Living."*

He takes a body, a location so small
he could barely be called a place;

and he grows like a seed from dry ground
to revive the pasture and become it,

extending the boundaries and filling
every clay jar with fruit from his vine;

containing all the nations
and cultivating their variety;

and sustaining celestial bodies
by making room for them in his space.

All our dying is buried in him
and we open our eyes to the sunlight

at home in Christ himself the land
of the living in whom we see

the goodness of God forever
with all of us who breathe and are

raising full cups, together the body
breakable but growing here.

HIDDENNESS

Where is the cloudy neon sign
The audible astral adhan
The inner voice persuading
That you do not stand far off
And hide yourself in times of trouble?

All the non-resistant non-believers
Ask to see with opened eyes
The one who might be standing in the garden
Among the trees and planets
Answering too quietly for them to hear.

Blind to unsurpassable greatness
My deficiency is reason
My disfunction is cognitive
And I cannot grasp what I cannot hold
And I cannot want to see you more

Or, less than a blunt demonstration
Is just what shapes my soul for wanting
To believe behind the trees
In subtle depth and freedom
Seeking to let what will be done

Not mine
Which cannot grasp what it cannot hold
Or hear beyond the planets revealing
All the seekers' hearts inscrutable
Walking in the garden with you, hidden.

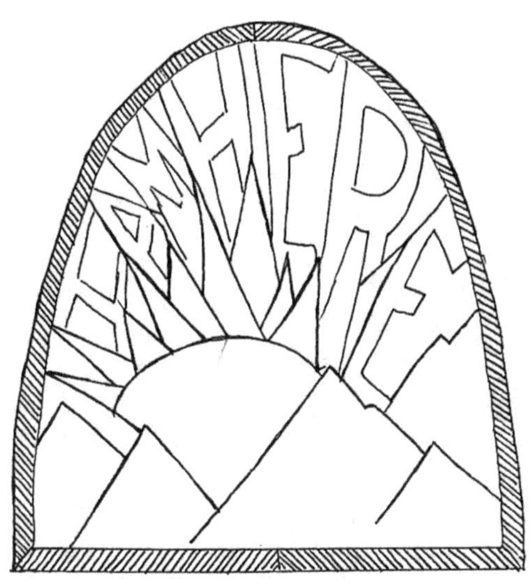

NOW

You remembered me, didn't you
All those moments ago?
But I am not there any more,
And neither are you

Here in this current present
That keeps on slipping slipping slipping
Into the future I must wait
And find him present

Who was timeless before
The temporal becoming
First without succession, then after
Everlasting enduring that much longer.

History might have been fixed-
A finished caravan of occurrences
Or open, possibly, broken, necessarily
Counterfactually A, inevitably B

But I think we know that you know
What will be. And that I am free
In this world actualized in the middle
At least a little better than the other ones

Where you are inside the moments
Enough to know that it is 3:39 and
Too early for the glass of wine we will
Enjoy when it is later for both of us.

So I hope for impermanence to end
And trust you remember me now
And then before the hour is past
You will say that it is finally time.

1:39

I can't be present in all of space
like you. So, what is left for me?

Mostly anywhere and sometimes
more relation than substance,

always a little farther than I realize
and less here than you,

I wish I could fill the whole cup
and still see the sunrise up close.

I can barely see you seeing me
in the evening swirling

a glass of wine that matches your sky
and my reflection in it trembling

as your great eye closes for the night
so we can stop seeing

until morning.

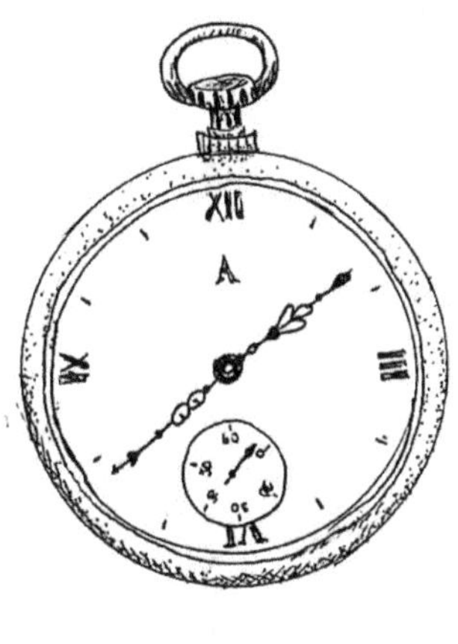
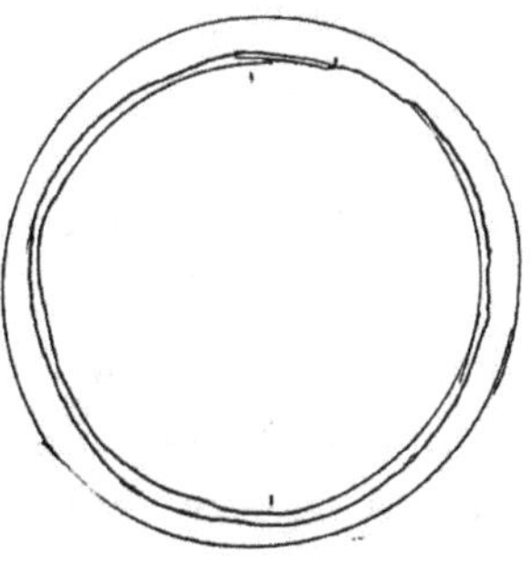
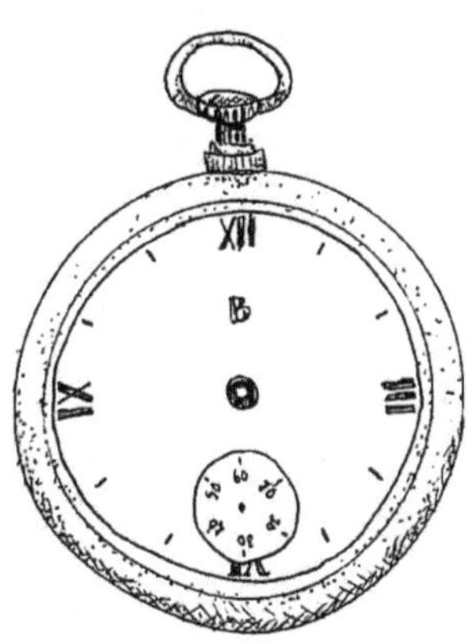

THE FATHER GIVES HIS SON CELLS

Unbroken perfect eternity
Acquires dimensions,
Limits, boundaries, edges
Front, back, top, bottom,
Inside and outside of everything

Infinite God becoming-
Starting small and getting bigger
Taller, stronger, wiser, better
Tasting, hearing, smelling, feeling
Friendship and decay and death

The omniscient is
Obscure, unknown, unknowing
Sleeping, eating, crying, bleeding
Surprise and sorrow arriving and leaving
The room, the planet, the land

Where he is planting and sowing
Perishable seeds of an undying kingdom
That grows in unbroken dimensions
Getting bigger, closer, wider, deeper
Until the broken undoer of dying cells
Comes home

FOUR WISPS

I

A charcoal tablet transfigures
painted pebbles of orthodox incense
into molten imagination
and my pent up prayers
bubbling in the terracotta burner
on the altar-ed wooden shelf
in my office sanctuary where
smoke unveils a sacred kingdom
and the scent of centuries' devotion
speaks a better word than my buried cries.

II

Four wisps of smoke rising
like ritual and rope release
the bindings of earth for me
from the grip of warm clay:
consequences I could not carry
because I would be crushed beneath them;
time that cannot be retrieved
though I resent not having that power;
pain that could have been avoided
only at the expense of my soul;
and happinesses not mine to pursue
past the cloudy clarity of prayer.

Let them be received in Spirit hands
able to hold together what I must
let go.

PRESENCE

You sit with me in the dark
at the table
where wine spills
on my fingers
because I couldn't see
the glass or
the bread
torn for us to share

THE WINE REMEMBERS

The wine remembers
Being blood when it dripped
From the true vine

Before it reaches my lips
So I can imagine
Dying

And the bread proclaims
With crunch and tear
That it is body

And my soul laid bare
To be fed broken but
Rising

TO SINGING

I sometimes feel the Presence when we sing
While distant stars explode out in the dark
Following bright words on a shaded screen
As when a hammer strikes and hot iron sparks

Fly upward with my soul above the room
Crushed leaves decompose into ancient paths
Open to meaning buried in the tune
A blazing campfire resolves into ash

On the foreheads of saints gathered today
New life emerges in the spring from mud
We're seeking the one who makes us this way
In nature affection is drawn with blood

And sacrifice made of melody on
Bodies held in orbit by gravity

I SPEAK IN TONGUES

I speak in tongues
when no one is listening
and my soul needs to talk
to someone and be heard
like liquid gurgling as it pours
from a mostly full clay jar
in words I haven't really learned
and don't think I know
(maybe angels do)
to pray the urgent accumulating
things I probably should not
understand and cannot tell
because language is coarse
the spirit fine and my mind
wants the music hidden
between the keys and syllables
that no other audience could
appreciate or inspire.

MAKE ME AN ICON

Make me an icon in a grey stone house
Sacred colors brushed onto grainy wood
Panels imparted with truth and presence
Opened toward the fire in a living room.

Write me with peace on my face but not tired
A flash of gold in the background alone
To brighten a Spirit beam bringing life
To the rugged beige island around me.

Give me a robe, maybe faded maroon
With a little blue on the inside showing
And a deep brown espresso extended
To weary worshippers and connoisseurs.

Can my ringed fingers form the name of Christ
Blessing and proclaiming as true saints do
No flaming dragon but maybe a cat
Reaching for compassion and finding it?

Paint with the color of faithfulness wild
Unmercenary love untamed inspired
To add life to the living and trying
And to the dying a reason for faith

WAITING ON HOLY SATURDAY

I wonder about the in-my-place-ness of you

dying for me as if to invite me toward

a better version of myself loving like you

and wanting you with me now in this place alive.

Sometimes I try to make your shadow cover me,

arms outstretched while I pray alone and imagine

the darkness aligning with my hands and feet,

the sun eclipsed behind the cross casting your shape

on everything while I wait for the light to come back

around and make the shadow unnecessary.

SUNDAY

I woke up on Easter morning
remembering the long fast is finished,
so I can again drink a cup of coffee
with my leftover pork roast and potatoes;
and my soul unburies the truth
that none of my suffering is meaningless,
my effort has not been wasted,
and all the beauty I am learning
to appreciate is not vanity,
but rays of a rising sun making visible
the resurrector of all good things.

OVERSHADOW ME

Thousands of times I have prayed
the canticle to Christ
as a light to illumine and guide me.
But, I don't know if have ever wanted you
before today as a shield
to overshadow me
overcome me
conquer me
cover me
envelop me
bury me
gather me
outreach me
supercede me
see more than me
be more than me
transcend me
overtake me
outlive me
outshine me
overshadow me.

me christ under me christ over me christ as a light christ as a shield christ beside me on my left and my right this day be within and without me lowly and meek yet all-powerful christ as a light illumine and guide me christ as a shield overshadow me christ beside me on my left and my right christ as a light illumine and guide me in the mouth of each who speaks unto me christ under me christ over me christ as a shield overshadow me christ beside me be within and without me lowly and meek yet all-powerful

THE WORLD IN HIS HANDS

He cups the earth in his bare hand
hovering over the waves and shores
of a hard brown seed and sees
its foam green future folded within
the intricate curled up structures-
all that fragile beige radicle potential
locked in the dark in the dirt in his palm.
Some soil shifts in his loose grip
and slips through red fingers parting
and trembling yellow light shines on
black sprinkles shaken and falling
free onto white fields still blank
with uncertainty about the harvest.
Holding the seed the garden keeper
is powerless to make it grow and no
force could unfurl the primordial leaf
any faster than the natural process
of reliable persuasion will permit.
He can only cultivate the conditions-
the finely tuned variables of freedom
in which buried things fulfill destinies-
to root himself in the soil and die
and wait for something mortal to sprout
by the virtue of a chosen weakness.
So he kneels to plant and pray.

FISH TACOS

Another piece of fish baptized
in beer batter and sizzling oil
turning crispy golden brown
and lifted up emerging new
as a wisp of steam arises
like the Spirit who is pleased
with my kitchen sacrament
at home on Saturday creating
after six long days of work.

Hovering over the week now past:
night vigils with an addict friend
weathering the crashing waves;
counseling a couple seeking
the Spirit in their union breaking;
and waking to impart to others life
immersed in sacred presence
over good coffee and in it;
we are shaping the earth for daylight.

My fish tacos are an offering
on a very good day consumed
by the Spirit and my family
at the table, beloved daughters
and sons with tortillas and cabbage
made holy by meaning we give them
swirling with a glass of orange wine
as a drizzle of garlic aioli
anoints this body and its bread.

A PSALM FOR AUGUST

My soul cringes a little. It worries
that it might be cliché to admit that
I want to be received into the arms
of the Father- your fingers on my back,
your breath on my neck, and your chin
pressed to my shoulder holding me
like a good metaphor in a poem
that makes me not want to let go
and convinces me that I am loved.

When I imagine that embrace
long enough, I stop trying to find
myself anywhere else. I am here
and whole and no longer wondering
if I belong. My soul unfolds
like a crumpled straw wrapper
with a drop of water on the table
where I used to sit across from my dad
eating french toast with warm syrup.

I breathe you in for a long while
and then release the kind of sigh
that makes people ask what happened,
exhaling the dust of a distant country
and beginning to believe again
that I have always been at home with you,
where I can still be brand new, surrounded
and filled to remain here and set out
walking the long road as a son.

FOR COMMON CREATURES

We caught a brown lizard
Flickering fast and filling the cracks
Like a puddle of wax and a wick
In a shadowy niche of beige
Bricks in the sunlit stone wall
Outside the tall Barnabas Church.
She crawled into a broken place
Bowing through the space above
The bolted door much more open
To her than me and facing east
As a priest expecting dawn before
The flame has gone dark and worshipped
Among the iconic witnesses
Casting her sight upon what is
Created for light, a glory revealed
In the temple for common creatures.
We could not follow. And God let her go.

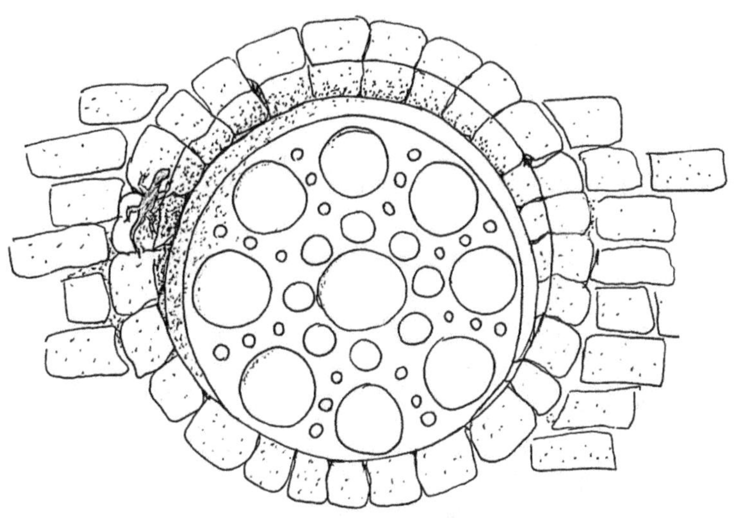

LOOKING FOR THE KINGDOM OF GOD

I'm looking for the kingdom
in July early morning haze
so I can live in it balancing

my favorite mug filled with coffee
in my left hand and in my right
the steering wheel of a scripture-

black Volkswagen freshly painted
after enough years of riding
through this ancient dust and gravel.

We're on our way to my daughter
Ruby's drivers license test.
She's studying the rules

I'm navigating the roads
trying to find the test location
and listening to poetry

podcasts and her questions
whose answers I sometimes know.
We're finding it together

in the beauty of things made new,
eventually. I take her hand
for a moment before we walk in.

SEEKING THE SPIRIT

Because a body cannot contain me
And my empty vessel must be filled
Like wind captured in an unguentarium
Submerged in oil wanting a way out
And a way in—like a slow swallow
Of hard liquor and power and meaning
Absorbed like flames into a night sky
With closed eyes and arms outstretched
Like paths inside reaching everywhere
Turning everything beyond itself within

WHERE THE SOUL IS

Descartes thought that he was
and that his thinking was
seated
in the pineal gland in the heart
of the brain,
but I am
standing
in the cloud of my consciousness
swirling around me making me,
a being thinking
with a brain and a body
like immaterial music
surrounding an ethereal player
who can touch the keys
with spirit fingers untouched
by the decay and by extension
the dimming of the song
that will keep playing
as me somehow
when the instrument fades
until he touches my hand
and strings
some new thing for me to play
for the rest of you.

ALL MY OIL IS IN ALABASTER

All my oil is in alabaster.

My heart breaks to touch the spirit

that drips from stone. Waves of life

flowing from a fragile vessel, breaking

from weakness. This brittle bottle

is filled to be poured out, revealed.

My emptying is inspiration

drawn from me in depth; worship

not strategy. I am a beautiful inefficiency,

valuable when spent, and broken

open in extravagance, uncontainable.

All my oil is in alabaster.

EKMEK

Ekmek means "bread" in Turkish
And "to sow"
For thirty years
Planting yourself in the soil
Praying for goodness to grow
From seeds of life
Buried sometimes too deep
For sprouts and branches to break
Through the surface of hard ground
Or benefit the birds and peoples
Until the harvest appears in time
For you to be ground into flour
Pressed raw into dough
And thrown to the flames
Rising to be shared
Around this wide table
In good company
Broken

EDITING BRANCHES

I have a friend who insists every year
on Palm Sunday that the crowd didn't
have palm branches, because there were
no palm trees in Jerusalem back then.

While we're laying down palm fronds
to find ourselves in the reverent crowd
welcoming the King who's come home,
his imagination is editing our branches,

switching them for something he finds
more historically accurate, but Jesus
Hosanna
looks down with whatever colored eyes
and steps graciously on his prickly branch.

THE ROCKS CRY OUT

Rocks have been crying out
for billions of years announcing
the presence of Christ in the heavens
he created ancient, vast, and
aggravating a tribe of men who try
to drown them out with angry shouts
as if theirs is the triumphal entry.

They need the earth to be young
enough not to threaten their sense
of superiority and flattened to fit
into narrow columns of text read
with pseudo-scientific seriousness
as if the whole world were a stone
small enough to throw at someone.

His glory cannot be contained
in clenched fists or fragile thought-
worlds revolving in circular orbits around
egos and answers neatly circumscribed.
His cosmos extends wide enough
to include them all with grace and bury
their pebble ideas under the millennia.

ESTHER

Esther's elbows scrape the painted pavement
lying face down holding onto her crown
to stare thinking into the dark hollow
of a live nuclear missile silo.

If only her husband were a better man,
a real king, not a drunk killing coward,
or Mordecai a wiser advisor
her people humble, gracious, less vengeful.

But such times as these make such
queens and souls
to stay the bloody ax of blunt empires
or at least divert the blade for today.
As the shape of a warhead is revealed

under the bare light of a cresting sun
she rises to face another darkness.

ELISHA AND HIS SERVANT

The ancient enemy Aramean army
had arrived in the night and surrounded
Elisha and his prophet companions
in the camp where they were working
on a tent wide enough for all his people.

He dipped a bit of barley bread
into a bowl of unknown stew and stood
to put a sure hand on a young shoulder
and show him they were not outnumbered,
pointing to the world behind the soldiers,

where after a whispered word of prayer
figures emerged from fire and fantasy:
many-eyed warriors stoic, strong-
hands like plows clenching curved swords,
riding six winged flame-beasts with tusks.

A glory fell on the holy company;
their eyes glowing fiercely like hot coals.
Flying axheads floated ready to strike
fear into mortal hearts and the enemy
who could not see them or anything else.

I checked my phone to see the time, but
put it back in my pocket to preserve
the sacredness of the present moment
and record in my memory the relief
and victory rising in my chest and face.

Elisha and I finished breakfast slowly,
at peace, amidst the glory and the chaos
of a blinded army and ten thousand
invincible creatures and their maker,
on our side as I took a sip of coffee.

SINKING JONAH

Inevitability crashes over me
like sea salt in my nose, exhaling
the deep and feeling a burn
that Nineveh will never know
while Tarshish fades in the horizon
that keeps bobbing and
disappearing out of focus.

Drowning in the doubt about
whether the world will wonder
why I did not know, and worse,
that they will know that
I wonder if I'm good enough,
which is the real stigma
among these sailors and fish.

In a splash of imagination
I see a door open wide
beyond the closing world
of seaweed and insecurity,
and it consumes me
with mercy and the smallness
of compassion withheld.

JONAH MOVES

While the prophet exile sleeps
Deeply
Lying down
Below deck
In the dark
With the rhythm of the waves
He moves.

After pagan panic awakens
Insecurity
Unreconciled
Sacrificing himself
For strangers
In the storm
He moves.

In a burial at sea
Resigned to
Seaweed and salt
Behind pain
And potential
While nations drown
He moves
God.

SAINT BARNABAS READS PRAYERS

Barnabas reads people's prayers
from a stone sarcophagus in a tomb
near the concrete house where I live

curled up taking refuge in a cleft
of the rock where Your hand hides me
while he unrolls tiny paper scrolls

wedged into cracks in his cove by other
pilgrims inspired to touch the source
of his gentle power to pull them out

into a blessed and better world:
Help me find my little pig t-shirt.
I would like to get married.

Ahmet is the kindest person
I have ever met. [a candle is lit]
Save us from the president.

I lay here with the incense breathing
hope of becoming another son
of encouragement and rest.

JESUS HEALS A PARALYTIC

There were no ropes
just a net of hands
to catch me in the stone
house that held the world
where he sat teaching
heaven to receive me.

I fell through the earth
and straw roof—a body
beneath the sky suspended
in a temple by a temple
and landed on holy ground
as a temple uncursed.

I stepped into the garden
restored and carrying
no shame on new legs
and the sea parted
astonished for me
and my four friends floating.

HE KNOWS WHAT LIES IN DARKNESS

"He reveals deep and hidden things; he knows
what lies in darkness, and light dwells with him."
Daniel 2:22

He knows what lies in darkness:
Shadows slipping into closets
With staccato steps whispering Conspiracy;
Clumps of envying lizard beings
Scraping the cloth beneath the mattress;
And all the hideous monsters hiding
In the deep of Nebuchadnezzar's nightmares—
Unspoken threats to power
And the power to unself kings.

He knows what lies in darkness.
The setting sun that curves past
The horizon of the knowable
Dwells with him as a light crown
Glinting off the mountain peak
Where no clouds obscure his reign,
Where rocks roll down to crumble
Corrupt regimes into dusty clay
And everything is revealed
And everything is his kingdom.

NANAIMO

Brown needles fall like anxious thoughts
on the trail I did not expect to walk today,

becoming path and past below me far
enough to watch them blur away.

New trees sprout from dying stumps,
as signposts leading to my clearing,

where the water in the lake is still enough
for every splash and echo, hearing

in them the Father's voice from sky
reflecting—I am loved. May it be enough.

THIS WEIRD GARDEN

Meaninglessness runs like razor wire
along the edge of reason's wall.
If anything is meaningless
everything is- excluding nothing
from its bloody isolation.

His sacrifice and her tears
Broken sunglass frames saved in drawers
Diamonds on the souls of her shoes
Ice cream that fills the cone
And Hopkins' Windhover

But once it has breached the broken wall,
Meaning floods the field undammed
Either everything is meaningless
Or nothing is- including anything
That sprouts in this weird garden

Shoulder freckles
The stickiness of dried apple juice
Leaves of grass, mosquitoes
Spinal meningitis
Every mile on the odometer and
Me

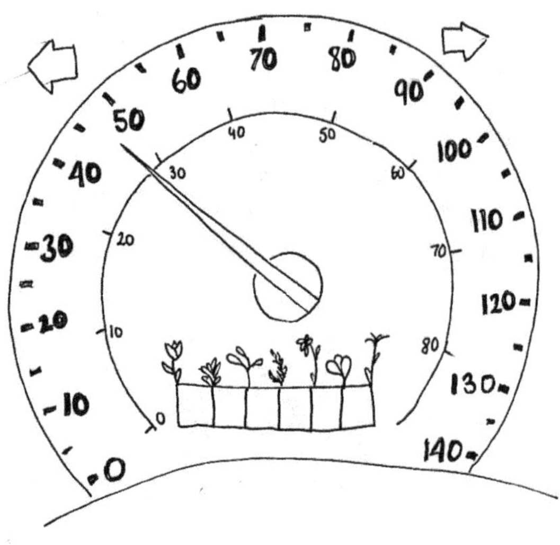

50
60
70
80
90
100
40
30
20
10
0
110
120
130
140
40
50
60
70
80
30
20
10
0

PORTSMOUTH PSALM

I wake up flying
over the Elizabeth River
arms outstretched
but not reaching for anything
more than the estuary
has already offered today.

Ripples flash beneath me
where your glory is reflected
in the August sun at my back
and a thousand invisible meteors
showering in season past the planet
on a path of their own,

and in the brackish water
caramelized from salt and fresh
flowing slower than I imagined
and awkwardly united like your
kingdom with this place. But here I am
floating between them

with the jellies pulled in by the tide
adapted just enough and just for now,
and the yellow crowned night heron
taking tall but careful steps
along the muddy creek bed until
you flood the banks again tonight.

I am flying satisfied and filled
with your breeze and in between
the sky and sea, the mud and the flow,
where I can still my eyes enough to see
even the crabs waving staccato
from the tall grass toward heaven.

FAMAGUSTA IN THE NEW CREATION

Will you uncrack the sidewalks in the new
Famagusta? And unclog the sewage pipe
that overwhelms my city with undersmells?
Make kind the cruel landlord living next door
where the broken clock on the wall marks time,
the kind he fills his long days with, judging
passersby and plotting tiny tyrannies
upon his tenants whose diversity
he increasingly resents. So, make more
colors and fill with variety the town
and her people until there isn't room
to squeeze in such narrowness of mind
like those winding streets in the old city walls
that I hope stay old. Unwind the razor wire
to set free all the empty fields to wander
and unsharpen the pain across the green
border dividing the island at the end
of two and a half miles of road that doesn't
have to separate the families and friendships
not yet made on the horizon where I want
the sunsets to remain just as they are.

WHEN I GET WHERE I'M GOING

When I get where I'm going
and the earth has been renewed

I will write in the shade
pterodactyls make

flocking in the heavens like liquid
leather, glory, teeth, and wings.

Little lambs and lions grazing
won't be made to feel small sharing

the valley with apatosaurus
stepping over them and stooping

low to reach the top of the tree
straddling the river and rustling

leaves like applause or poetry
trunk tail sway stanza bow.

And I will know that I am known
with triceratops and trilobites

who will be found with me
grateful, whole, and growing timeless.

NATURAL

Cruelty spreads in the field out there
As natural as the kindness where
Both buds and thorns, dirty, green
Spring alike from deep roots unseen

Untended earth for now gives way
As mean vines shoot up holding sway
Over good seeds destined to win
Through virtue's slow cultivation

The mortal fix a guarantee
That unkindness can only be
A temporary thriving thing
Till death plucks up evildoing

And life enduring spreads in me
Overtaking inhumanity
Whose roots corrode in restored ground
And all the kindness lost is found

ROCK COLLECTION

My daughter deposits a rock
into the round-topped treasure box
that guards her growing collection.
Thuds and rattles sound the value
of each piece to her and so to me.
What distinguishes these from those
scattered in the garden outside
isn't quantified by qualities
or colors or mineral compounds.
She likes them.
And that's enough for both of us.

She knows I keep rocks of my own.
A brown round one in my briefcase
gathered from a gravel driveway,
a stone altar to remember
losing a long season of love.
We look at it together sometimes
so she can share its worth with me,
a pebble three thousand miles from
the rubble heap, not because it shines,
but because we look at it sometimes.

And today, squinting from the sun
on my front porch and the planet
I'm learning to see the beauty
as Christ opens to me his treasure
composed of rocks, thuds and rattles,
heaps of things and shining people,

gardens and memories of loss,
a collection, a stone altar,
beautiful because he keeps it.
And we look at it together.

51

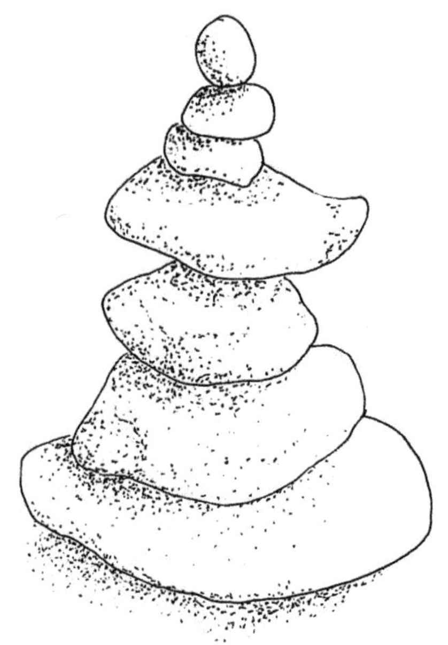

IC XC NIKA

Thick red drops paint the skull
Like a war helmet discarded
In defeat and left useless
On top of a hill at the bottom
Of a somber wood panel icon
On the wall of a church converted
By the latest regime
Into a museum of relics
Where the death of Jesus siezes
The passing faithful and the hill
In the faded sacred painting
Taking control of everything
In the temple where it hangs
And the land that changes hands
Around it and the whole island
And the people and powers
Of evil even beyond the sea
And the souls and very bones
Of those who already know
That he conquers not by killing
But by dying for his enemies.

DEATH IS AT WORK

"So then, death is at work in us,
but life is at work in you." 2 Corinthians 4:12

Death is at work in me
I can hear its promise faintly
The melody, the chorus, maybe one more verse
The terms, the conditions, the inevitable agreement
Encroaching, spreading, fulfilling
The cells and molecules made not to endure
An infection of impermanence

Death is at work in me
His song rises, a sacrifice
To drown out my soul's unfair terms and conditions
Hoping for eventual agreement
To encroach, spread, fulfill
A promise I can feel trapped in my cells and molecules
An impermanent sentence

Death is at work in me
But life is at work in you

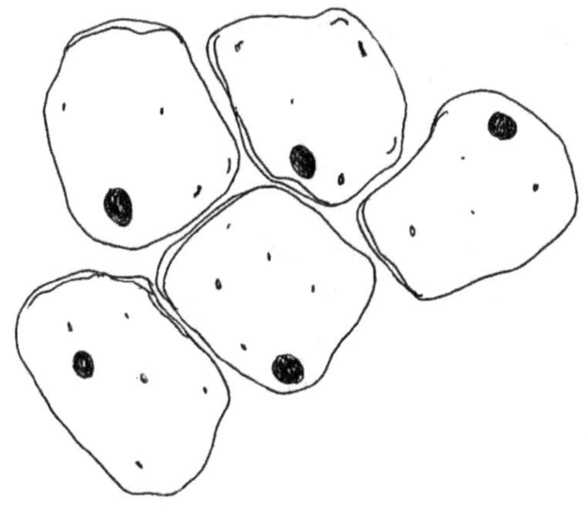

RESURRECTION

Is it a drop of wine left in the glass
Rehydrated in the morning,
A swirl of water to reconstitute
Dried compounds in perfect proportion?

Or is it a fresh pour into an empty glass
Of a better vintage absent flaws—
Balanced, intense, complex
And longer than I can now appreciate?

Or is it seven billion unfinished glasses
Returned to the one amphora source
Where molecules mingle in unity
As a field blend perfect in uniqueness?

THE END

God doesn't love you
The way a carpenter loves a hammer
for smashing parts together
to build one more table in Bethlehem;
or the way a chess player loves the bishop
for accomplishing strategic captures
to exploit the rules and rule the board;
or the way a musician loves the trumpet
for producing a beautiful tune
to announce the glorious end
of an unresolved symphony.
You are an end, human, not just a means;
a victory, not just a strategy;
not the expense, but the reasons
for building a table where we can sit
one day in Jerusalem
together in conversation
that needs no justification.
He loves, and therefore the world is,
and is in balance between the good
of the kingdom plan and the beloved
sons and daughters without sacrificing
either to a calculation
of instrumental usefulness
or production value.
So let the trumpet sound
for those of us who know we play
for good in a production without end.